D0596611

...if you sailed on the

Mayflower

...*if you sailed on the*
Mayflower

by ANN McGOVERN   **Pictures by J. B. HANDELSMAN**

SCHOLASTIC BOOK SERVICES
NEW YORK · TORONTO · LONDON · AUCKLAND · SYDNEY · TOKYO

For M. F. — and a crazy carousel

The author acknowledges with thanks
the invaluable assistance given by
Arthur G. Pyle, Education Director
Plimoth Plantation, Massachusetts

This book is sold subject to the condition that it shall not be resold, lent, or otherwise circulated in any binding or cover other than that in which it is published — unless prior written permission has been obtained from the publisher — and without a similar condition, including this condition, being imposed on the subsequent purchaser.

ISBN: 0-590-08738-X

Text copyright © 1969 by Ann McGovern. Illustrations copyright © 1969 by Scholastic Magazines, Inc. All rights reserved. Published by Scholastic Book Services, a division of Scholastic Magazines, Inc.

18 17 16 15 14 13 12 11 10   9/7 01/8

Printed in the U.S.A.

07

CONTENTS

The New World

Plymouth

The First Thanksgiving

Poop deck

Captain's cabin

Quarter deck

Rudder
(for steering)

Flour

Barrels of water

General supplies

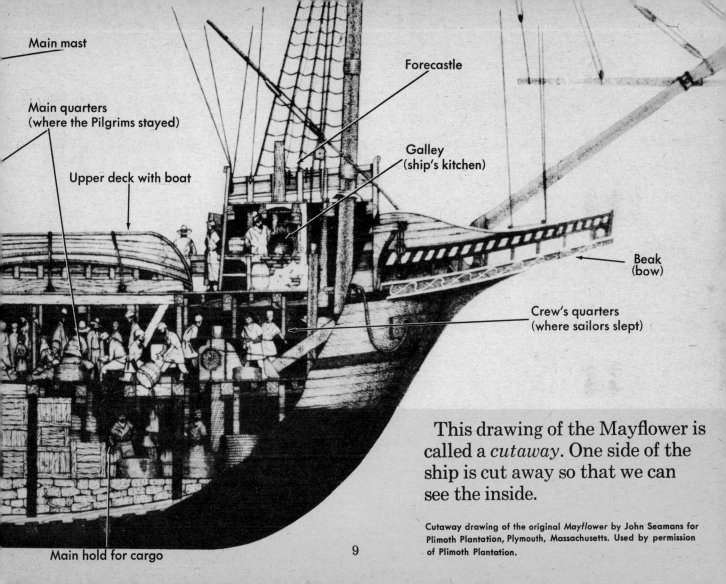

Main mast

Main quarters
(where the Pilgrims stayed)

Upper deck with boat

Forecastle

Galley
(ship's kitchen)

Beak
(bow)

Crew's quarters
(where sailors slept)

Main hold for cargo

This drawing of the Mayflower is called a *cutaway*. One side of the ship is cut away so that we can see the inside.

Cutaway drawing of the original *Mayflower* by John Seamans for Plimoth Plantation, Plymouth, Massachusetts. Used by permission of Plimoth Plantation.

9

The Pilgrims

A *pilgrim* is someone who goes on a long, long journey.

The people on the Mayflower were leaving their homes to sail far away to a new land, a new life. They were going on a long, long journey, and so we call them Pilgrims.

Where does the Pilgrim story begin?

In England, many years ago, everyone had to obey the rules of the King's church. There were some Englishmen who wanted to have their own separate church. They were called *separatists*. They had secret church meetings.

The King found out about the secret meetings and he put some of the men in prison.

Now the separatists were afraid to stay in England. They went to Holland in 1608. There they could worship God as they

pleased. They lived in Holland for twelve years.

Life in Holland was not easy. The men had to work very hard. They made very little money.

And they were worried. They did not want their children to forget how to speak English. They did not want their children to become soldiers and sailors for Holland.

What could they do? Perhaps they could go to the New World, some of them thought. These are the people we call Pilgrims today.

The Pilgrims needed a ship to take them to the New World. They bought a ship — the *Speedwell* — in Holland. But the *Speedwell* was small and old. They would need a second ship too — a bigger and better ship. But where would they get such a ship? They didn't have any more money.

At last they made an agreement with some businessmen in England. The businessmen got them a ship — the *Mayflower* — and bought some food and supplies.

13

In return, the Pilgrims had to agree to work for the businessmen for seven years. The Pilgrims promised to send furs and lumber from the New World. Then, after seven years, they could begin to work for themselves.

The Pilgrims thought the agreement was not fair, but that was the only way they could get to the New World.

They sailed the *Speedwell* from Holland to England where the *Mayflower* was waiting for them.

On the *Mayflower*

The *Mayflower* was a sailing ship. The ship moved when wind filled the sails.

And the *Mayflower* was a cargo ship. She was made to carry cargo — things like cloth and hats and barrels of wine.

She was not made to carry people. But the *Mayflower* did bring one hundred and two people from England to make their home in the New World in the year 1620.

The *Mayflower* was a good, strong sailing ship. She was about ninety feet long — about as long as two big trailer trucks. And she was a clean-smelling ship, not like most ships of that time.

For twelve years, the *Mayflower* had carried a cargo of wine on her voyages. Little by little, some wine slowly leaked out of the wine barrels. The wine took away the bad smell of garbage.

How many people sailed on the Mayflower?

Too many people!

The *Mayflower* carried about thirty sailors and one hundred and two passengers. Thirty-four of them were children.

There were not supposed to be that many people on the *Mayflower*. Some passengers were supposed to sail to the New World on the smaller ship, the *Speedwell*, but something went wrong.

The two ships had begun their voyage from England together on August 5, 1620. But the *Speedwell* was leaky and had to go back to shore.

Some of the passengers from the *Speedwell* stayed behind in England. Others crowded onto the *Mayflower*.

Before the ship reached the New World there was a new passenger on board!

A baby boy was born as the *Mayflower* sailed across the Atlantic Ocean. Guess what his parents named him. *Oceanus!*

Who sailed on the Mayflower?

A doctor, a soldier, a shoemaker, and a blacksmith were on board. There was a cooper too. His job was to look after the barrels of beer and water and to make sure they did not leak.

Most of the passengers were farmers or weavers or shopkeepers. And there were some servants on board the *Mayflower*. They were hired to do the hardest work in the New World.

19

Some men brought their wives and children along. Some men sailed without their families.

About thirty-five of the passengers were going to the New World because they could not worship God in their own way in England.

Other passengers were going because they could not find work in England.

Others were going to the New World for adventure.

Were the people on the ship friends?

Some people were. Some people weren't.
The sailors hated the Pilgrims. And the Pilgrims didn't like the sailors.

The sailors made fun of the Pilgrims who got seasick. They called them "glib-gabbety puke stockings." One sailor said he wanted to throw half the Pilgrims into the sea.

The sailors hated the Pilgrims' prayers and holy songs. The Pilgrims didn't like the sailors' bad language.

But at the end of the voyage, the sailors had to admit that the Pilgrims had plenty of courage.

And the Pilgrims were thankful that the sailors got them safely to the New World.

What could the Pilgrims take with them?

Not much.

Each family could take a Bible box for the family Bible, and a chest for their clothes and other belongings.

Mothers with babies could take a cradle for the baby to sleep in.

Women could bring the things they would need for cooking.

Men could bring their guns, swords, and tools. They brought tools for building houses and tools for working in the garden.

Whatever did not fit in the chest had to be left behind. If you sailed on the *Mayflower*, you would have to leave almost all your toys behind.

What would you eat and drink on the Mayflower?

Day after day, you would eat the same kind of food. You would not like it the first day, and by the last day you would be sick and tired of it.

Most of the time you would eat *salt horse* and *hardtack*. That's what the sailors called it.

Salt horse was their name for salted beef or pork or fish.

Hardtack was a hard, dry biscuit.

There were dried peas and beans, cheese from Holland, and some butter.

To cook their food, the Pilgrims would have had to build charcoal fires in metal boxes called *braziers*. But most of the time the

weather was so stormy that it was too dangerous to have a fire. So most of the time the Pilgrims ate cold food.

There were barrels of beer and barrels of water. But after standing in the barrels for a while, the water was not safe to drink. So everyone drank beer — even the children.

The Pilgrims had to look out for bugs in their food. Every ship in those days had bugs crawling everywhere.

By the end of the voyage, the biscuits got harder. The cheese got moldy. The butter turned bad. Even the beer began to go sour.

Where would you sleep?

You would have to sleep on the floor (called a *deck*) with about eighty other people, below the main deck. There would be hardly any light and hardly any air.

There was not enough sleeping space for thirty sailors and one hundred and two passengers.

Some people slept in a small boat called a *shallop*. The shallop would be used for exploring trips later.

Captain Jones let about twenty important passengers sleep in his cabin. He took a smaller cabin for himself.

The sailors slept at one end of the ship. A few of the sailors may have slept in hammocks, but most of them slept on the deck.

Would you be able to keep clean?

You would not be able to keep clean. There were no bathrooms on the *Mayflower*. If you wanted to wash, you would have to wash in salty water from the sea.

Most likely you would wear the same clothes day after day, night after night, for sixty-six days and nights.

At the end of the long voyage, your clothes would be torn and dirty — and smelly too.

Was it a safe voyage?

It was dangerous for one small ship to make such a long voyage. In those days one ship almost never sailed alone.

One small ship alone on a huge ocean. What would happen if the *Mayflower* were shipwrecked?

What would happen if they ran out of food and supplies?

Who would get word to England?

Storms were a danger.

The *Mayflower* sailed in good winds and good weather for about a month. Then, in October, strong winds began to blow. The *Mayflower* tossed and rolled in the waves. The tossing and rolling made most of the passengers seasick.

Just as everyone was feeling better, another storm broke. This one was worse than the last. Above the howl of the wind and the crash of the waves came the sound of something breaking.

The main beam had cracked!

The deck was in splinters!

Water poured down on the Pilgrims crowded below. They were soaked. So were their clothes, their bedding — even their food.

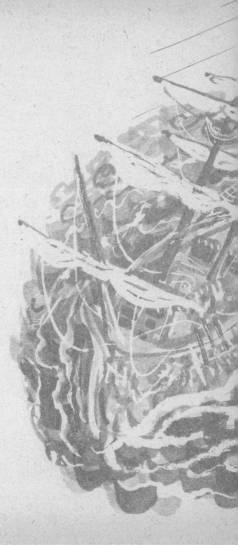

The ship might have sunk. But someone remembered the great iron screw they had brought from Holland. The Pilgrims were going to use it to help build houses in the New World. Now they used it to help keep the beam in place.

Sickness was a problem.

One day, the doctor's servant, young Will Butten, took sick. He had ship's fever. The doctor could not help him, and Will Butten died.

Many people were getting sick. Now even the sailors prayed. They prayed for the end of the terrible voyage.

Would you have had any fun
on the Mayflower?

It might be fun to watch the sailors. And you could play with the dogs. There were at least two dogs on board.

And there was a cat. Every ship had a cat to catch the rats.

There were plenty of books to read — if you liked grownup books. One of the Pilgrim leaders, William Brewster, brought along many books.

If you liked to sing, you would have fun singing. The Pilgrims sang *Psalms* — religious songs — every day.

*Would you get into trouble
on the* Mayflower?

If you were like John and Francis Billington,
you would.

The Billington boys were always getting
into trouble.

One day, Francis Billington set fire to a
piece of rope. He was standing close to some
barrels of gunpowder.

If just one spark from the rope had gone
into the gunpowder — BOOM! You would not
be reading this book. For that would have
been the end of the *Mayflower*, the end of the
Pilgrims, and the end of our story.

The Pilgrims said it was God's mercy that
saved them that day.

The New World

It was the morning of November 9, 1620. The Pilgrims saw a sandy beach. They saw trees and bushes.

They had reached Cape Cod, in what is today the state of Massachusetts. Now there is a town — Provincetown — at the very place the Pilgrims landed.

The voyage took sixty-six days — counting from September 6, the day the *Mayflower* left the *Speedwell* behind and sailed from Plymouth, England.

How did the Pilgrims feel
when they saw land?

William Bradford, one of the Pilgrim leaders, wrote:

"Many fell upon their knees, and blessed the God of Heaven who had brought them over the vast and furious ocean."

The Pilgrims were full of joy. But they must have felt frightened, too, as they looked across the water to the lonely shore.

They had sailed thousands of miles across the sea. They might never again see their homes in England.

Here, in this strange land, there were no homes. There were no towns. There were no friends to greet them.

They would have to stay on the *Mayflower* until they could find a place to live, until they could build houses.

The passengers began to quarrel. Some of the Pilgrims said that when they got to shore they would go wherever they pleased. "None have the power to command us," they said.

The Pilgrim leaders knew that they must all stay together for safety. They had to make laws that would end the quarreling.

What were the first laws the Pilgrims made — even before they left the ship?

In the Great Cabin of the *Mayflower,* the Pilgrims drew up an agreement. It was the first set of laws in America that said the majority should rule. It was called the Mayflower Compact.

The Mayflower Compact promised fair laws. It gave the people the right to choose their own leader.

Forty-one men signed the Mayflower Compact. Then they voted to have their governor, John Carver, be governor again for the next year.

What was the first thing the Pilgrims did when they got on shore?

The women washed clothes. There were so many dirty clothes to be washed! It took the women all day to get those clothes clean.

The children ran! After weeks and weeks of being cooped up like chickens and crowded in like sardines, it was wonderful to run and run and run on the beach.

Some of the men began to repair the shallop which had been banged about in the storm. Some began to explore the countryside to look for a place where the Pilgrims could live.

What did the Pilgrims find on Cape Cod?

The Pilgrims made three exploring trips on Cape Cod to look for a place to live.

On one of the trips, they found a basket of Indian corn. The Pilgrims needed corn to plant so that they would not go hungry the next year. But they knew the corn belonged to the Indians. It was not theirs to take.

At last they decided to take as much of the corn as they could carry. They said they would pay the Indians back later.

Why didn't the Pilgrims stay on Cape Cod?

Some of the Pilgrims wanted to stay. The Indians had cleared the land for planting. There were ponds of fresh water. There was plenty of fish.

These men said they should not waste another day looking for a better place. It was almost winter. Many people were sick. Food was almost gone. They must start building homes before it got too cold.

Other Pilgrims said no. The water along the shore was not deep enough for ships to come and go. There were too many Indians. The fresh water was in ponds, and ponds dry up in summer. Surely there must be a better place than Cape Cod.

Back and forth went the arguments. At last the Pilgrims decided to make one more exploring trip. This was to be the last chance.

What happened on the third exploring trip?

Only the Pilgrim leaders and the strongest men left the *Mayflower* and set out in the shallop—eighteen men in all.

The wind howled. One of the Pilgrim leaders, Edward Winslow, wrote that "the water froze on our clothes, and made them like coats of iron."

When the sun went down, they sailed to the nearest beach. They saw Indians cutting

up a big blackfish — a kind of whale. But the Indians ran away when they saw the Pilgrims.

That night the Pilgrims saw the Indians' fire miles away. But in the morning there were no Indians to be seen.

The next night, around midnight, they heard a loud cry. The Pilgrims fired off their guns. The cry stopped as suddenly as it had started.

Somebody said it must have been wolves.

In the morning they heard the same awful cry they had heard in the night.

Wolves in the morning? Impossible.

Then arrows began to fly. Indians!

Miles Standish fired a shot. The Indians yelled. It sounded to William Bradford like, "woath, woach, ha ha hach waoch."

Arrows flew. Guns roared. Soon the Indians ran away.

The Pilgrims set out in the shallop again.

"After some hours sailing," Bradford wrote, "it began to snow and rain. About the middle of the afternoon the sea became very rough. They broke their rudder and it was as much as two men could do to steer with a couple of oars."

One of the men shouted, "Be of good cheer. I see the harbor."

But the storm grew worse. The mast broke and fell into the sea.

They were heading straight for rocks. The men turned the boat around just in time.

Soon they came to an island, and the next morning, Saturday, the storm was over. But the men were too tired to do much work. They

made a fire, cleaned their guns and rested.

Sunday they spent the day in prayer.

On Monday they were up before the sun. Then the eighteen men sailed away from the island to try once more to find a landing place on shore.

In a while they reached land. It was December 11, 1620. They had come to Plymouth, the place Captain John Smith had discovered and named six years before.

Did they land on Plymouth Rock?

No one knows for sure.

The rock we now call Plymouth Rock was the only good landing place along two and a half miles of sandy beach. Many people think that must be where the Pilgrims landed.

*Why did the Pilgrims decide to stay
in Plymouth?*

There were running brooks, and fields already cleared for planting.

There were two rivers.

The harbor was safe for small boats.

And they saw no enemy Indians.

The eighteen Pilgrims sailed the shallop back to Cape Cod to tell the others about Plymouth.

And on December 16, 1620, the *Mayflower*, with all the Pilgrims, sailed to Plymouth.

Plymouth

How did the Pilgrims plan to build their town?

The Pilgrims decided to have one street that would go from the shore to the top of the hill.

The top of the hill was a good place for their big guns — their cannons. From there they could see the countryside. They could look out across the sea.

The Pilgrims planned to build houses along both sides of their street. They named the street First Street.

The Pilgrims could not build houses for everyone that first year. So they worked out a plan. The men who had no wives or children would move in with families. Some of the

smaller families would move in with larger families. The houses would be crowded, but everyone would have a roof over his head.

The land was measured. A plot of land was given to each family. Larger families were given more land than smaller families.

What was the first building in Plymouth?

The first house the Pilgrims built was the Common House. At first it was used as a storehouse for tools and as a shelter for the men who were working. Later that year it was used as a church and even a hospital. Guns were kept there too.

The men and the boys began to chop down trees. They sawed pine logs to make planks. They split cedar trees to make clapboards for the Common House.

Most of the men went back to the *Mayflower* to sleep. A few stayed on shore to watch over the tools.

Many days the weather was so bad the men could not work. Because of the bad weather it took the Pilgrims twenty-six days to build the Common House.

Did they work every day?

From Saturday afternoon until Monday morning, no one did any work — not even cooking.

That was the Pilgrims' time to worship God. They prayed, sang Psalms, and listened to William Brewster's long sermons.

This made Captain Jones and his crew angry. Captain Jones wanted to work every day. He wanted to help the Pilgrims get settled as fast as possible so he could sail the *Mayflower* back to England.

How did the Pilgrims spend their first Christmas?

They worked. Christmas came on a Monday that year. And Monday was just another working day.

The Pilgrims did not believe in having a Christmas holiday.

So for the Pilgrim children, there were no Christmas trees, no Christmas stockings, no Christmas presents, and no Christmas songs.

But the sailors had a good time. They sang and drank beer.

What was one of the biggest problems in Plymouth?

Sickness. There was terrible sickness in Plymouth that first winter.

There were some days in February when only six or seven people were well enough to take care of the ones who were sick.

By spring, about half of the Pilgrims and sailors were dead. Three whole families died during this terrible time.

The brave little group of Pilgrims sadly buried their dead. They did not mark the graves in any way. They hoped the Indians would not find out how few Pilgrims were left alive. They were afraid the Indians would attack if they knew.

Did the Pilgrims have any medicine?

No medicine could cure the terrible sickness. But the Pilgrims had plenty of medicine to cure aches and pains.

Plants called *herbs* were the medicine of the Pilgrims. When spring came, the women planted herbs in their gardens.

Suppose you cut yourself. Your mother would make a medicine from the *wild daisy*. She would mix it with animal fat and smear it on your cut.

Suppose you had a headache. Your mother would mix ground-up *sage* with fat and

Hyssop

Chervil

Sage

Rose

cornmeal. You would have to eat it, even if you hated the taste.

Rose leaves and the fruit of the rose, called *rose hips*, were said to be good for almost anything. Today we know that rose hips have the same vitamins oranges have.

If herbs did not cure you, you would go to Dr. Fuller. Most doctors of that time thought a good way to cure the sick was to bleed them. Dr. Fuller would cut open a vein in the sick person's arm and let some blood flow out.

Who were the Pilgrims' first friends?

Indians were the Pilgrims' first — and best — friends.

On March 16, 1621, three months after the Pilgrims landed at Plymouth, a tall Indian walked into the village.

He was "stark naked," wrote Edward Winslow, "only a leather about his waist."

"Welcome, Englishmen," the Indian said, and he held out his hand in a friendly way.

The boys and girls of Plymouth had never seen an Indian before. Now an Indian was standing right next to them! And he was speaking English! His name was Samoset.

He told the Pilgrims that he had learned English from visiting English fishermen.

He told the Pilgrims all about the Indian tribes nearby. The place the Pilgrims called Plymouth was called *Patuxet* by the Indians. About four years before, a strange sickness had killed everyone in the Patuxet tribe.

But there were other Indians nearby. Samoset himself was visiting the Wampanoag Indians, ruled by wise Chief Massasoit.

Samoset spent the night in Plymouth. When he left, the Pilgrims gave him a knife, a ring, and a bracelet.

Two days later, Samoset was back. He brought five Indians with him — five hungry Indians. The Pilgrims gave them food, and in return, the Indians sang and danced.

Samoset came back four days later. This time he brought along an Indian named **Squanto**.

Squanto stayed in Plymouth. He stayed with the Pilgrims for the rest of his life.

It was lucky for the Pilgrims that he did. Squanto was the Pilgrims' best friend.

What did the Pilgrims learn from Squanto?

Squanto showed the Pilgrims where the fish swam, and how to catch them. He showed them where to hunt deer, turkey, and other animals.

He showed them where the wild plants and herbs grew — and how to use herbs to make their food taste better.

He told them when to plant corn.

He showed them how to plant their kernels of corn in little hills, along with three fish in each hill to make the corn grow better.

How did the Pilgrims and the other Indians get along?

The Pilgrims could "walk as safely in the woods as on the highways of England," wrote Edward Winslow.

Squanto helped to arrange a meeting between Chief Massasoit and Governor Carver.

Chief Massasoit came to Plymouth with twenty Indian braves. He wore a chain of white bone beads around his neck. His face was covered with oil and painted a dark red.

All the Indians were painted — some black, some red, some yellow. Some of the Indians wore animal skins.

The Pilgrims and the Indians greeted one another. They ate and drank together.

Then Chief Massasoit and Governor Carver got to work on a peace treaty.

What were the terms of the peace treaty?

The Pilgrims and the Indians made some agreements.

The Pilgrims and the Indians promised they would never attack each other.

When the Indians came to Plymouth, they would leave their bows and arrows behind, they said. And when the Pilgrims visited the Indians, they would leave their guns behind.

There would be no stealing. Each would help the other if an enemy attacked.

The peace treaty was not put in writing, but peace between the Pilgrims and the Indians lasted for fifty-four years.

Would you live in a log cabin?

No. The Pilgrims had never even seen a log cabin.

The houses they built in Plymouth were the same kind of houses they had lived in back in England. But the houses in Plymouth were much smaller. They had steep roofs, covered with a kind of straw called *thatch*.

There was no glass in Plymouth. The windows were made of paper or cloth. The paper or cloth was rubbed with fat to let some light in.

The first houses had only one big room with a room upstairs, called a *loft*. Some people slept in the loft.

Where would you sleep?

You would have to sleep on the *Mayflower* until your house in Plymouth was finished.

Some people lived on the *Mayflower* until the end of March, almost four months after the Pilgrims landed in Plymouth.

When your house was finished, you would sleep on the floor until you had time to make a mattress.

You would sleep on the mattress until you had time to make a bed. Beds for grownups were made first. Grownups put their mattresses on top of rope springs.

You were lucky if you were one of the few Pilgrims who had a featherbed. Featherbeds were linen bags filled with soft goose feathers. In the summer time, you could sleep on top of it. It made a soft mattress. In the wintertime you could sleep under it. It made a warm blanket.

Small children slept in a bed called a trundle bed. The trundle bed was kept under the grownups' big bed during the day. At night it was pulled out.

Babies slept in cradles.

Children seven years old or older slept upstairs in the loft.

What kind of furniture did the Pilgrims have?

The first houses did not have much furniture. There was not much room for furniture. And there was not much time to make it.

For a table, the Pilgrims put wooden boards across two wooden sawhorses. At night they put the boards against the wall so that they would have room to put their mattresses on the floor.

Not every house had a real chair. When there was a chair, the man of the house used it. Everyone else had to sit on a bench or on the floor — or stand up.

A big fireplace took up one side of the room. It was used for cooking, for light, and for heat in the wintertime.

Some people brought rugs from England. They used them to cover their beds. They never put them on the floor.

You would hang your everyday clothes on pegs on the wall. Guns and helmets were hung on pegs too.

Your Sunday clothes would be kept in a pine chest, along with the sheets and blankets.

What kind of table manners were the children taught?

Children ate standing up at the table all through the meal. It was good manners to keep your hat on while you ate.

You could not say a word at the table unless a grownup spoke to you first.

It was good manners to eat with your fingers. There were no forks in Plymouth and only a few wooden spoons. Clam shells were often used as spoons. You would use the same knife to cut meat that you used to cut wood.

In some homes, the cooking pot was put right on the table. Into the pot would go your clam shell — or your fingers — to take out your food.

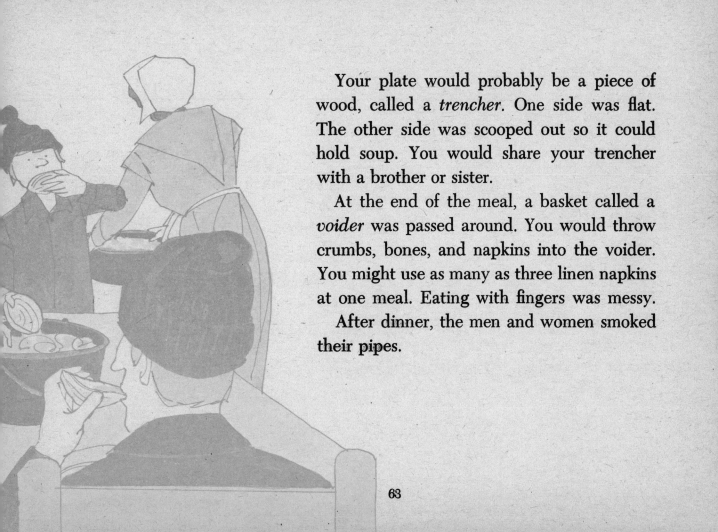

Your plate would probably be a piece of wood, called a *trencher*. One side was flat. The other side was scooped out so it could hold soup. You would share your trencher with a brother or sister.

At the end of the meal, a basket called a *voider* was passed around. You would throw crumbs, bones, and napkins into the voider. You might use as many as three linen napkins at one meal. Eating with fingers was messy.

After dinner, the men and women smoked their pipes.

Do you think that Pilgrim men always wore black clothes and tall, stiff black hats?

Do you think that Pilgrim women always wore long gray dresses with white collars?

Well, they didn't. Those were just their Sunday clothes.

The Pilgrims wore brightly colored clothes for every day.

Women wore long woolen dresses of red, green, or blue. They wore white linen caps that came down over their ears.

Girls dressed just like their mothers.

Pilgrim men and boys wore long-sleeved blue or green shirts. They wore woolen or leather jackets called *doublets* and pants called *breeches*. They wore red or green woolen stockings and knitted stocking caps.

Little boys wore long dresses until they were six years old. After that, they dressed like the men.

On cold days, the Pilgrims wore red or purple capes. Women and girls wore capes with hoods.

In the summer, children and many grownups went barefoot.

The only clothes the Pilgrims wore that first year were the clothes they brought with them on the *Mayflower*.

Were there special jobs for boys and girls?

Yes. Boys watched the cornfields. One or two boys sat on the corn-watching stand. They took along a pile of stones to throw at any bird or dog or wolf who might get into the cornfield. Boys took turns watching the field until the corn began to grow.

Boys and girls both shelled corn. The kernels of corn were scraped off the cob along the edge of a shovel or against the long handle of a pan.

Cooking a turkey was an all-day job for a boy or a girl. An iron rod called a *spit* went all the way through the turkey. The handle of the spit had to be turned until the turkey was cooked on all sides. It was hot work. And it took from nine in the morning till four in the afternoon.

Another job was mattress making. Boys and girls put pine needles or corn husks or feathers into linen bags.

Boys and girls gathered special grasses to make thatch for the roofs of the houses. They had to walk miles to the banks of the creek where these grasses grew.

They picked mussels from the rocks in the water. They dug for clams in the mud.

Boys helped build houses. They helped hunt for food. They made wooden pegs which were used instead of nails.

Girls helped cook and serve the meals. They helped with the washing.

Boys and girls were as busy as the grown-ups. There wasn't much time for fun.

Did children go to school?

There were no schools in Plymouth that first year. Everyone was too busy to bother about school.

But you would learn to read. You would learn your ABC's with a kind of book called a *hornbook*.

The hornbook was not a real book with pages. It was a piece of wood with a piece of paper on top of it. The ABC's were printed on the paper. Then a thin sheet of horn was put on top of the paper to protect it. You could see right through the horn.

Not everyone in Plymouth knew how to read or write. Those who knew taught the others.

Boys and girls learned to read the Bible. There were no storybooks for children in Plymouth. If you liked to read, you had to read the same books as the grownups.

What rules did people have to obey?

Everyone had to obey the rules made by the leaders of Plymouth.

The most important rule was going to church on Sunday. Everyone had to go.

Everyone had to work hard.

It was a crime to get drunk.

And stealing was a crime.

Did people break the rules?

The first year, only three people were arrested for breaking the rules.

The people of Plymouth had to take turns watching the town for dangers.

One night it was John Billington's turn to stay up all night. He was supposed to look out for fires or strange Indians. But he said he would not do it.

John Billington was arrested. The Governor told Billington what his punishment would be. His neck and his heels would be tied together.

When Billington heard this, he said he would take his turn watching Plymouth, like everyone else.

The Governor let Billington go free.

But John Billington kept on getting into trouble. Nine years later, he shot a man and was hanged for his crime.

The two servants of Steven Hopkins got into a fight. They fought with sword and dagger.

The Pilgrim leaders were angry. There were not enough men left in Plymouth, they said. No one had the right to risk his life in a fight!

The two men would have to be punished. Each man would have his head tied to his feet. They would stay tied for a whole day. And they could have nothing to eat.

After an hour of punishment, the men cried to be let free. Mr. Hopkins took pity on his two servants. He asked the Governor to let them go. And the Governor did.

What happened to the Mayflower?

On April 5, 1621, almost four months after landing at Plymouth, Captain Jones and his crew sailed the *Mayflower* back to England.

Captain Jones said he would take any of the Pilgrims who wanted to go back with him. But not one Pilgrim went back.

The Pilgrims had been through terrible times. They would stay together now — no matter what might happen.

The First Thanksgiving

Were there special days for fun?

Weddings were fun for the whole town. The first wedding in Plymouth took place in May, five months after the Pilgrims landed.

The Pilgrim's first Thanksgiving in the New World was a special time for joy.

What did the Pilgrims have to be thankful for?

They "had all things in good plenty," wrote William Bradford.

The corn had grown well. There was plenty to eat. If they were careful, no one would go hungry the next winter.

Seven houses were finished. More were being built.

The danger of sickness was over.

The Pilgrims did not have to be afraid of Indians. The Indians were their friends.

But most important, they had done what they had set out to do. They had found a place to live where they could worship God in their own way.

And so the Pilgrims decided to set aside a special time to give thanks.

What day was the first Thanksgiving in the New World?

Thanksgiving was not one day. The first Thanksgiving holiday lasted for three days. It took place around the middle of October in the year 1621.

Who took part in the holidays?

Everyone in Plymouth — about fifty Pilgrims and their Indian friends.

The Pilgrims were thankful for their Indian friends. Without the Indian corn, the Pilgrims would have starved. Without Squanto to teach them Indian ways, the Pilgrims could not have lasted the year.

The Governor of Plymouth asked Chief Massasoit to come. The Governor told the Indian chief to bring along a few friends.

Chief Massasoit brought more than a few friends. He showed up with ninety Indian braves!

What did they eat for Thanksgiving?

When you think of Thanksgiving, do you think of turkey and cranberry sauce and pumpkin pie?

The Pilgrims had turkey too. But their turkeys were not like the ones we eat today. Their turkeys were wild and much bigger.

Plenty of cranberries grew around Plymouth. But the Pilgrims did not make cranberry sauce.

They had plenty of pumpkins, but no pumpkin pie. They did have meat pies.

There were wild geese, wild duck, lobsters, eels, clams, oysters, and many other kinds of

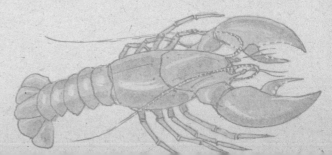

fresh fish. And the Indians killed five deer for the feast.

There was corn cooked in many different ways. And there was popcorn too.

The Pilgrims had no sugar. Perhaps they used wild honey to sweeten their food.

There were vegetables from the Pilgrims' gardens — carrots and cucumbers, turnips and onions, radishes, beets, and cabbages.

Most of the cooking and all of the feasting was done outside. Deer, turkeys, geese, and ducks were roasted on outdoor spits. Lobsters and oysters were roasted over hot coals.

For dessert there were wild berries and fruits. Strawberries, gooseberries, plums, cherries, and other fruits had been picked in the spring and dried to eat later.

No one went hungry the first Thanksgiving. There was so much food that it took three days to eat it all!

How did the Pilgrims spend Thanksgiving?

The Pilgrim women and girls spent most of their time cooking.

The men and the boys played games. The Indians and Pilgrims shot bows and arrows. They played "throwing the bar" and hand wrestling. They had contests — jumping and running and racing.

They played games of *stool ball* with a leather ball filled with feathers.

Miles Standish held a parade. One man blew the trumpet. One man beat on the drum. The little group of soldiers marched and fired their guns.

Thanksgiving was a time for eating and drinking, a time for playing and for having fun.

And for the Pilgrims, it was a time for sharing and for giving thanks to God.